Look Up!

PHASE 3 AND 4

/oi/ear/ /air/

Level 4 – Blue

BookLife

Helpful Hints for Reading at Home

The graphemes (written letters) and phonemes (units of sound) used throughout this series are aligned with Letters and Sounds. This offers a consistent approach to learning whether reading at home or in the classroom.

HERE IS A LIST OF PHONEMES FOR THIS PHASE OF LEARNING. AN EXAMPLE OF THE PRONUNCIATION CAN BE FOUND IN BRACKETS.

Phase 3			
j (jug)	v (van)	w (wet)	x (fox)
y (yellow)	z (zoo)	zz (buzz)	qu (quick)
ch (chip)	sh (shop)	th (thin/then)	ng (ring)
ai (rain)	ee (feet)	igh (night)	oa (boat)
oo (boot/look)	ar (farm)	or (for)	ur (hurt)
ow (cow)	oi (coin)	ear (dear)	air (fair)
ure (sure)	er (corner)		

HERE ARE SOME WORDS WHICH YOUR CHILD MAY FIND TRICKY.

Phase 3 Tricky Words			
he	you	she	they
we	all	me	are
be	my	was	her

Phase 4 Tricky Words			
said	were	have	there
like	little	so	one
do	when	some	out
come	what		

TOP TIPS FOR HELPING YOUR CHILD TO READ:

• Allow children time to break down unfamiliar words into units of sound and then encourage children to string these sounds together to create the word.

• Encourage your child to point out any focus phonics when they are used.

• Read through the book more than once to grow confidence.

• Ask simple questions about the text to assess understanding.

• Encourage children to use illustrations as prompts.

PHASE 3 AND 4

/oi/ear/ /air/

This book focuses on the phonemes /oi/, /ear/ and /air/ and is a blue level 4 book band.

How many words can you list with oi in?

Look up at night. How far can you see, high up in the air?

Can you see the stars? You might see stars on a clear night.

Stars

Stars are big bits of gas that burn.
They are boiling hot!

Star

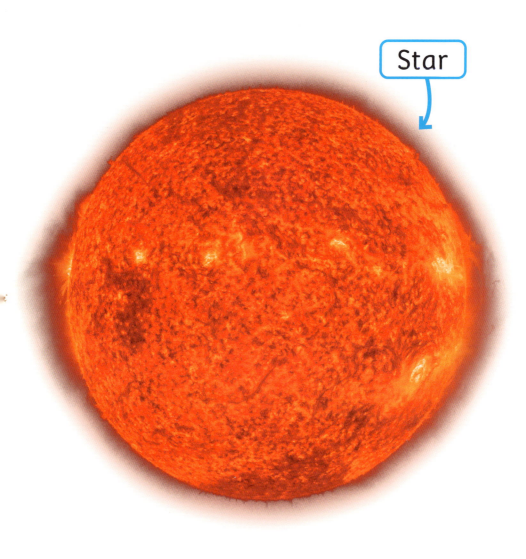

Lots of stars are far from us, but a big star is near to us.

The Sun is a star. We get light from the Sun. It helps us see.

Part of the planet is light. Part of the planet is dark.

Light

Dark

At night, we do not see the Sun.
We see the Moon.

Can you point at the Moon?

The planet we are on has one moon.
The Moon has no air.

I will go to the Moon in my rocket gear! Will you join me? Have no fear!

Saturn is a big planet. It has a lot of rings.

Can you point to the rings?

Mars has a pair of moons. You might see Mars at night as a red dot in the air.

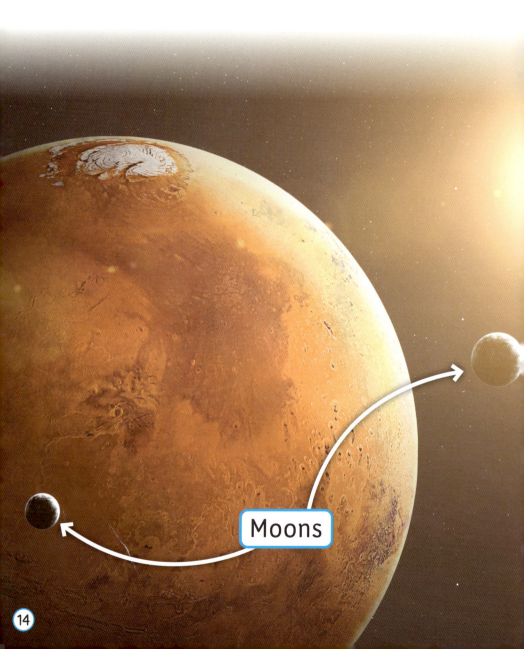

Moons

Mars is not far from us, but we will not go to Mars for years.

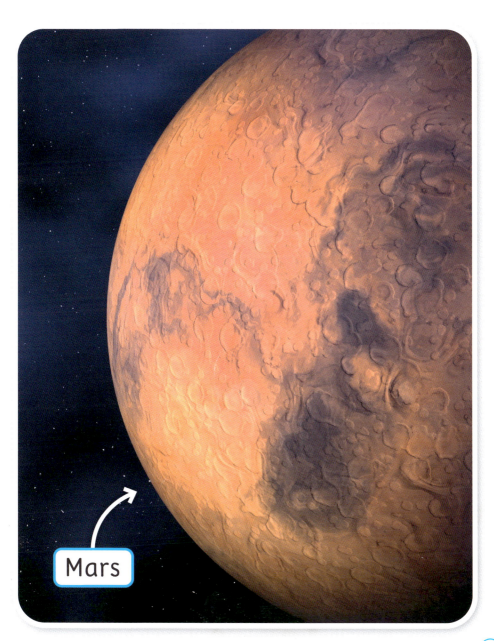

Mars

©2021 **BookLife Publishing Ltd.**
King's Lynn, Norfolk PE30 4LS

ISBN 978-1-83927-900-3

Look Up!
Written by William Anthony
Designed by Drue Rintoul

An Introduction to BookLife Readers...

Our Readers have been specifically created in line with the London Institute of Education's approach to book banding and are phonetically decodable and ordered to support each phase of Letters and Sounds.

Each book has been created to provide the best possible reading and learning experience. Our aim is to share our love of books with children, providing both emerging readers and prolific page-turners with beautiful books that are guaranteed to provoke interest and learning, regardless of ability.

BOOK BAND GRADED using the Institute of Education's approach to levelling.

PHONETICALLY DECODABLE supporting each phase of Letters and Sounds.

EXERCISES AND QUESTIONS to offer reinforcement and to ascertain comprehension.

CLEAR DESIGN to inspire and provoke engagement, providing the reader with clear visual representations of each non-fiction topic.

AUTHOR INSIGHT:
WILLIAM ANTHONY

Despite his young age, William Anthony's involvement with children's education is quite extensive. He has written over 60 titles with BookLife Publishing so far, across a wide range of subjects. William graduated from Cardiff University with a 1st Class BA (Hons) in Journalism, Media and Culture, creating an app and a TV series, among other things, during his time there.

William Anthony has also produced work for the Prince's Trust, a charity created by HRH The Prince of Wales, that helps young people with their professional future. He has created animated videos for a children's education company that works closely with the charity.

PHASE 3 AND 4

/oi/ear/ /air/

This book focuses on the phonemes /oi/, /ear/ and /air/ and is a blue level 4 book band.

Image Credits Images are courtesy of Shutterstock.com. With thanks to Getty Images, Thinkstock Photo and iStockphoto. Cover – Yaroslav Vitkovskiy, LightField Studio, Bonezboyz. 3 – Africa Studio, Fototocam , Zerbor , Somchai Som.4&5 – xtock, Sergey Mironov. 6&7 – NASA images. 8&9 – Aphelleon, MarcelClemens. 10&11 – Triff, Just Super. 12&13 – Tomsickova Tatyana, Paopano. 14&15 – Orla, Vadim Sadovski.